Christian Liberty Nature Reader

Book One

Written by
Florence Bass

Revised and Edited by
Wendy Kramer

Christian Liberty Press
Arlington Heights, Illinois

A publication of

Christian Liberty Press

502 West Euclid Avenue
Arlington Heights, IL 60004

Printed in the United States of America

Preface

This reader is designed not only to improve a child's reading skills and comprehension, but also to increase the youngster's understanding of and delight in God's wonderful creation.

This text also seeks to expand the vocabulary skills of the reader by way of special drill in the key terms in **dark print** found throughout the book. Instructors are encouraged to make sure that each student understands the meaning of these vocabulary terms in the text. A helpful listing of definitions for each of the key terms is found at the end of the book under "Words You Should Know."

The Bible says that we are to do "all for the glory of God" (1 Corinthians 10:31). Reading for God's glory necessitates reading material that draws attention to Him and His truth, reflects His majesty, and meets the standards of the Holy Scriptures. What this means is that we should take any reading selection to Philippians 4:8 and ask these simple questions: "Is it true? Is it noble? Is it right? Is it pure? Is it lovely? Is it admirable? Is it excellent? Is it praiseworthy?"

As we look at the American readers of days gone by we find that the biblical standard was followed. Such readers featured the finest British and American authors who emphasized God, morality, the wonders of creation, and respect for one's country.

The *Christian Liberty Nature Reader Series* follows the pattern of the past. Believing that the student can gain an enhanced appreciation for God by studying His creation (Psalms 19:1, Romans 1:20), this textbook seeks to present the majestic splendor of His handiwork.

It is our prayer that this series will give the reader the joy that is to be associated with "good reading," and that the knowledge imparted will help "make wise the simple" (Psalm 19:7).

Michael J. McHugh
Curriculum Director

TABLE OF CONTENTS

To Mom

For the first eight to ten years of a child's life the field or garden is the best schoolroom, the mother the best teacher, creation the best lesson book.

With leaf and flower and tree, and with every living creature, from the leviathan of the deep to the speck of dust in the sunbeam, we can learn from each the secrets of its life.

Teach the children to see the glory of Christ in all of nature. Take them out into the open air, under the noble trees, into the garden; and in all the wonderful works of creation teach them to see an expression of His love.

As Basil the Great, bishop of Caesarea, has said, "If you speak of a fly, a gnat, or a bee, your conversation will be a sort of demonstration of His power whose hand formed them; for the wisdom of the workman is commonly perceived in that which is of little size. He who has stretched out the heavens, and dug out the bottom of the sea, is also He who has pierced a passage through the sting of the bee for the injection of its poison."

A Nest of Harvest Mice

Harvest mice have long tails which help them to hold on to stalks of plants so they do not fall.

A Little Mother

Children, did you ever think about how much your mothers do for you? They give you good things to eat, clothes to wear, and help to make a pleasant home for you.

God also made mothers for many of His tiny **creatures**. He made these mothers to care for their little ones, just as your mother cares for you.

Mud Wasp

One little mother is the **mud wasp**. She works very hard. She never seems to stop for a minute. What can she be doing? Just now, she is building a nest. She comes with a little ball of mud. She spreads this mud with her jaws. She begins in the middle and spreads it down one side of the nest. Then she darts away. She has gone for more soft mud. Soon she comes back with another piece. She begins at the top and spreads it out on the other side.

Making a Nest

This mud wasp is building her nest. What a noise she makes as she works! Soon she will have one room done.

Then she will go in and lay a little egg. After that, she must find something for her baby to eat when it creeps out of its egg.

What do you suppose she brings? She brings little spiders! As many as eight spiders may be put in for one baby wasp to eat.

The mother wasp walls up the spiders in a room with her egg. She makes many more rooms like this. Then she flies away and never comes back. She never sees her own little ones. She has given them all the care that they need.

The Little Children

What happens inside the mud wasp's nest? The eggs she has laid are still at first. Soon it is time for them to **hatch**. A tiny white **grub** creeps out of each egg. It looks like a little worm.

A worm creeps out of an egg? Yes! That is just what a baby wasp looks like. It eats the spiders that its mother left for it. It grows bigger very fast.

After a while it goes to sleep in a little case. It seems to be dead, but it is not. It is only growing to be a wasp like its mother. By and by it wakes up—a full-grown wasp. It never grows any more. It bites a hole through its mud house and flies away.

Do you think the wasp knows how much its mother did for it? We cannot tell. We do know that each new mother wasp will care for its own little ones. God the Father made them to follow His plan.

The Paper Wasp

God made the mud wasp to build her house of mud. Another wasp, the **paper wasp**, builds her house of paper.

Where does a wasp get paper? She does not find it. She does not buy it at the store. She makes it herself!

The paper wasp chews bits of wood off of old fence rails or fallen trees. She bites the wood chips into tiny pieces to make paper.

The paper wasp builds her nest under a bridge or the edge of a building. This protects her home from wind and rain.

Each room, or **cell**, in the nest is closed at the top, but open at the bottom. When the wasp has finished working on her nest, she lays an egg in each cell.

A Social Colony

A paper wasp is different from a mud wasp in several ways. She builds her nest of paper, instead of mud.

The paper wasp is a **social** insect. This means that she is a bug that lives and works with her family. The mud wasp lives and works alone. She is a **solitary** insect.

When a mud wasp closes her eggs up tightly, her work is finished. She has given her babies food and a home. They will grow up alone.

A paper wasp does not fly away when her eggs have been laid. She must work hard when her eggs hatch. When the babies, or **grubs**, creep out, their mother must feed them. She brings spiders and insects for them to eat. She is very busy finding food for all of her children.

When the babies grow big enough, each cell is closed off tightly. The babies sleep as they change into adult wasps.

The Children Grow Up

The baby paper wasps have grown up. They look just like their mother. They do not fly away from the nest. They stay to form a **colony**. A colony is a group of insects that live together.

There is a lot of work to be done. Old rooms have to be cleaned up, so more eggs can be laid. New rooms must be built. When the next group of eggs hatch, there will be more babies to feed. The mother paper wasp has plenty of help now. Her grown up children can clean, build, and search for food. If there is danger, the wasps will also fight to protect their nest.

While the **weather** stays warm, the colony grows. When the weather turns cold, many of the wasps will die. In the winter, each wasp sets off alone. It finds a crack or hole where it can hide. While the weather is cold, it does not even come out for food. It does not need to eat when the weather is so cold.

When the weather grows warm, each mother wasp comes out. She will build a nest. She will start her own colony.

The Digger Wasp

The **digger wasp** is another hard working insect. She does not build her nest out of mud or paper. She lays her eggs under the ground.

How does a wasp get under the ground? She digs a hole with her front feet, like a dog! When the hole gets deep, she must carry each piece of dirt up and out, as an ant does. When she finishes her **tunnel**, she lays an egg.

The digger wasp flies away to find food for her baby. She brings back a fat caterpillar. She closes it in the hole with the egg she has laid.

When the egg hatches, the baby wasp looks like a worm. It will eat the food that its mother has left for it. The baby is safe in the hole. It has plenty to eat until it changes into an adult wasp.

The digger wasp is a **solitary** insect, like the mud wasp. It grows up alone. Later, it works and lives alone. God made the wasps to live this way. His plan is perfect for them.

Spiders

Have you ever seen a spider on her **web**? She is an amazing creature.

A spider has eight legs. It has two body parts. Some spiders are gray or brown. Other spiders have beautiful red, orange, yellow, or other colored **markings**.

Jesus gave spiders a special way of doing things. They are able to **spin** webs out of **silk**. Spiders have **spinnerets** which make this silk.

Spiders' webs are very sticky. Insects fly along and do not see the fine threads. They become stuck in the spider's web. The spider eats the insects that it catches in its web. Is it not wonderful that God has made so many different, and interesting creatures for us to study?

The Spider Meets a Man

A spider sat beside her web. She was waiting for an insect to get stuck on the sticky threads. Instead, a man came along. The spider did not want to see him.

The spider shook her web as hard as she could. Maybe she thought this would keep him from seeing her. She was afraid that the man would kill her.

Maybe he would, too. But it would be a foolish thing to do. The spider is one of man's best friends. She is a help to him every day. She eats many insects that are **harmful** to people, or to the plants he grows. Most spiders do not harm people, either.

Finally, the man went away. The spider sat still again, waiting to catch a bug to eat.

Mrs. Spider and Mrs. Wasp

Mrs. Spider sits quietly on her web. Suddenly, she sees a mud wasp flying very fast toward her. The spider is not happy to see Mrs. Wasp. Do you remember what the mud wasp brings for her babies to eat? She brings spiders!

The spider is wise enough to know that she is in danger. She drops down from her web. As she goes, she spins a line to climb back up to her web. Now she lies very still upon the ground. She has beaten the wasp. Even if Mrs. Wasp could see the spider lying on the ground,

she would not touch it. The spider is playing "dead." She is all curled up in a little ball. This will keep her safe. The mud wasp will not bother with a dead spider. She can not give a dead spider to her babies, so off she flies.

The Mrs. Spider is lying on

the ground, playing dead. She waits until she is sure that the wasp has flown away. Finally, she climbs up her **silken** rope to her web. Again she sits and waits. She hopes that an insect will come flying along. If he does not see her web, he may be caught in it. That is the way that the spider gets her food.

Some people think that spiders are scary. Others think that they are cruel. All living things have a part in God's plan. Spiders eat insects. Even if we do not like spiders, we must be thankful that they eat many harmful insects.

A Spider in a Flower

There are many different kinds of spiders. One little spider does not build a web to catch her dinner. She hides in a flower instead. You cannot see her, unless you look very closely. She is almost the same color as the flower that she sits upon.

Does she know colors? How can she tell which flower looks just like her? She seems to know, because she never goes to a flower of the wrong color. Why is the color of the flower so important to this spider?

There are two reasons. First, the spider does not want to be seen by her **enemies**. They might jump on her and carry her away.

Also, she does not wish to be seen by the little insects that come to the flower to feed. She holds still so she looks like a part of the flower. When an insect comes close enough, she can jump up and catch it for her dinner.

The Lord Jesus is the One who gave the spider her pretty color. He also taught her to use a flower to catch her food.

A Spider Takes a Balloon Ride

A tiny spider wanted to go on a long trip. She could not drive a car. She could not get a ride on a bus or an airplane. Instead, she used the very special gift God gave her. He showed her how to make her own balloon and fly away!

First, the spider climbed to the top of a plant. Next, she made her legs and her body very hard and straight. She began to spin a lot of light, **silken** threads. They were so light, they floated. Soon she had spun so many threads, she felt they

Up in a balloon

Spider (enlarged)

Gathering in thread for descent

Just before taking flight

could carry her. She gave a little leap, and away she sailed through the air. The spider was so light, the wind rushing against the many threads was enough to make her float up and away!

The spider can ride on the wind for a long way. When she wants to come down, she just rolls up her threads. Her own weight can now take her down.

Only God could plan and create such a wonderful creature.

A Mother Spider

Just as there are many kinds of wasps, there are also many kinds of spiders. They live their lives in ways that are different from each other.

One mother spider is very careful with her young. Before her babies are born, she carries them around! She lays hundreds of eggs and puts them in a **sac**. It looks like a ball. This spider is so careful of her egg sac, that she will fight to protect it. She will lose one of her legs rather than her babies. She is very brave.

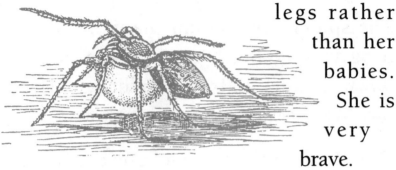

When the little spiders hatch out, she still cares for them. Sometimes they ride around on her back! The little spiders grow very fast. Soon their **skins** are too small for them. They grow new skins under the old skins, and lose their old ones. Soon they will be able to care for themselves. Until they grow up, their mother will watch over them.

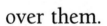

A Spider Builds a Bridge

A little spider sat on a bush beside a brook. She wanted to get across the water. She did not know how to fly or swim. There was no bridge for her to run across. The wise spider knew just what to do.

She began to spin. Soon, a soft silken line floated gently over the stream and stuck to

a bush. That was what the spider hoped would happen. If her first line had not gone across the water, she would have tried again.

The spider ran over her silken bridge. She spun another line as she went. At the other side she made the thread tight. Back and forth she went, making her bridge stronger each time. Soon it was finished. Spiders have built bridges this way for many years.

There is a story about a man who wanted to build a bridge. He sent a kite over a river to get the first line across. Do you think that a spider gave him the idea?

A Spider Under the Water

This is the story of another spider. Strange to say, this spider is a **diver**.

Why would a spider want to dive? She dives to get to her home. Her home is under the water!

How can a spider live under the water? She has to have air to breathe. First, she builds a little house out of silk. Then she brings bubbles of air down with her and fills up her home.

She makes her egg **sac** and lays her eggs.

She raises her babies under the water. It

seems like a strange way for a spider to live. God knew it would be the best way for her to raise a family.

A Spider Under the Ground

Many spiders live in webs strung on plants and buildings. Other spiders have different ways of building their homes. We have learned about a spider that lives under the water, and about another that lives in a flower.

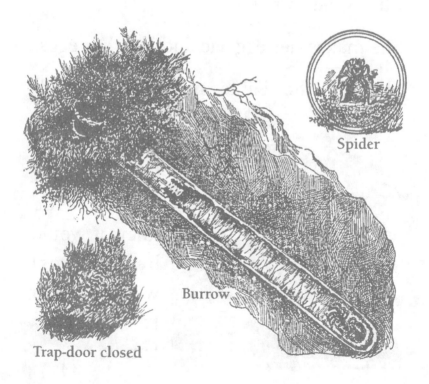

Spider

Burrow

Trap-door closed

There is another spider that builds her home under ground. She digs a round hole down into the earth. This hard working spider even covers the mud walls of her home. She

The Trap-door Spider

spins her silk and carefully lines the **tunnel** with it. Then she makes a door that just fits into the top of her house. She holds them together with a **hinge**. She makes the door a little larger at the top than at the bottom. This is so it can not fall in on her. She covers the inside of this door with silk, too.

The spider can not leave the outside of her **trapdoor** mud-colored. A bare spot of dirt in the weeds could be seen by other creatures. Birds or wasps could find the spider's home. They might kill her or her babies.

The wise spider gathers plants like those nearby. She covers her mud door with them. Now her home is very hard to find. She and her babies are safe. This special spider is often called the "trapdoor" spider.

Evening Chorus

Summer is a busy time for animals. Insects, birds, frogs, and other creatures must work hard. They gather food and build their homes. They lay eggs and care for their babies.

In the evening, you can hear the sounds made by many of these creatures. It is like an evening **chorus**. You do not have

to pay to hear the music. Just step out
into your backyard and listen!

Thousands of crickets chirp together like an **orchestra**. Frogs call out their mating songs. Some have songs that are smooth and quiet. Others, like the bullfrog, call out like a horn honking. You may also hear owls screeching or hooting.

In the summer, one insect even gives off light! The firefly darts around the yard. He is like a tiny flashlight turning on and off.

Enjoy the sounds and sights of a summer night. They are like a **concert** given by God's creatures.

Butterflies

Tiny white butterflies can often be seen in a garden in the summer. They look like **snowflakes**, or little flowers. Often, they **flutter** around the cabbages. Do they like to eat cabbage? No, they are too **dainty** for that kind of food.

A butterfly lands on a leaf. Then it darts off to another cabbage and stops on another leaf. Each time a butterfly lands, it leaves a tiny, green egg. Later, a little green worm will creep out of each egg. It does not look at all like its pretty mother.

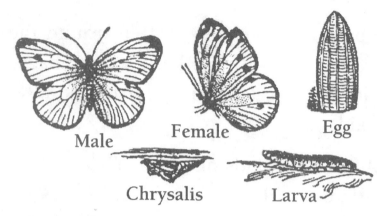

Male Female Egg

Chrysalis Larva

A butterfly's baby is a **greedy** thing. It loves to eat cabbage. Its mother knew that a cabbage plant would be a good place for it to hatch. The little worm eats so much that it grows very fast.

Finally, the worm stops eating. It grows sleepy. A thin, green skin covers it, and the worm does not move. After a few days, it breaks out of its shell. It has become a beautiful white butterfly like its mother.

It sounds almost like a make-believe story, but it is true! Jesus made these tiny creatures. He gave them their amazing way of growing up.

Honey Bees

Here is a little **honey bee** on a big **sunflower**. What is she doing? She is brushing the flower with tiny hairs on her legs. Yellow dust called **pollen** is on the flower. The bee makes the dust fall off of the flower. She has tiny folds on the back of her legs, like baskets. She catches the pollen in these baskets.

What will the bee do with the yellow dust? She will take it home to make **beebread** for the baby bees. She lives in a **beehive**. Inside the beehive is the **honeycomb**. It is made up of little cells, or rooms. Each one has six sides.

The bees fill many of these rooms with sweet honey. They make the honey from **nectar**. The bees gather both nectar and pollen from the flowers.

The **worker** bees are very busy. The food they make feeds the whole colony. Without the worker bees, the **queen** bee, her husband—who is called a **drone**, and their babies would die.

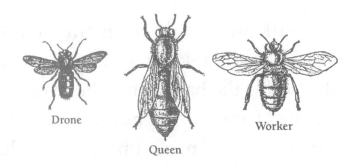

Drone

Queen

Worker

The Beehive

The inside of a beehive is an interesting place. The worker bees have many jobs. Some of the bees make the **wax** cells that make up the honeycomb. They also make beebread to fill up some of the rooms.

The bees all pet and care for their queen. She is the mother of all the bees in the hive. She lays eggs in the cells prepared by her workers. Most of the **larvae** that hatch from the eggs are fed beebread. Beebread is made from pollen and honey. Only a few of the **females** are fed royal jelly.

This special food makes the bees grow up to be queens!

When a new queen bee comes out of her cell, there may be trouble. There can only be one queen bee in each hive. The new queen and the old one may fight until one of them is killed. Sometimes, a group of the worker bees goes off with one

of the queens. This is called a **swarm**. They will start a new colony.

Bees are hard working creatures. One of the things they work so hard at is making honey. They need it to live through the winter. Bees make much more honey than the colony will need. Beekeepers gather the extra honey from the hives. People can enjoy the bees' honey, too!

The Cicada

The **cicada** is another interesting insect. It lives under the ground for seventeen years! How does the insect get under the ground? Why does it want to live there?

An adult cicada laid her eggs in a twig. Later, the egg hatched. After six weeks, the cicada baby dropped down from the tree. It dug down under the ground. There it lived for many years. It would suck juices from the **roots** of the tree for its food.

Seventeen Years

For seventeen years, a cicada lives among the tree roots. Suddenly, it knows that the time has come to leave the ground.

The cicada drills its way through the dirt. It climbs up into a tree. It fixes its **claws** into the bark. A very strange thing happens. The cicadas' skin **splits** open along its back. The insect pushes its way out of its own outside **shell**. It leaves behind a shell that looks like a little, empty bug.

The cicada is very weak when it first comes out of

its shell. It has soft, green wings. The cicada waits and rests. Soon the **delicate**, green wings get larger. They become harder, and turn black.

Now the cicada can fly among the trees and find a mate. The cicadas' song is high and loud. You can hear its song on long summer days.

Not a Locust

Many people call the cicada a **locust**. A locust is a very harmful insect. It causes great damage to crops. In the Bible, we read about God sending locusts as a **curse** upon the **Egyptians** for their sin of not obeying Him.

The cicada is not nearly such a pest as the locust, but it can cause damage to fruit trees. When the cicada lays its eggs

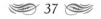

in the tiny branches, they often break. People sometimes wrap their trees with cloth when they know the cicadas are coming.

When cicadas come out of the ground, there can be thousands of them in a small area. They crawl into each tree by the hundreds. It is very strange to see the many, many empty shells that they leave behind, clinging to the branches. It seems funny to us; insects stepping out of their own outside shell! God made so many interesting creatures for us to study.

A Basket Maker

God has made many insects that have special ways of doing things. He made one little moth that knows how to build a basket. The moth lives inside of the basket.

(section of female chrysalis)

Caterpillar and Basket

When the moth first hatches from its egg, he is a caterpillar. He immediately begins to build a little basket right around himself. As he grows, he makes the basket bigger. He builds it by reaching out to grab bits of things from the ground or a branch. He attaches these pieces to his home. He carries his basket everywhere. When he is scared, he creeps inside and shuts the door. When he needs to eat, he crawls almost out of the basket. He always keeps a tight hold on his little home.

One day, the caterpillar falls asleep. When he wakes up, he will fly away. He has turned into a moth!

This moth's **mate** never leaves her home. She has no wings, so she cannot fly. She lays many little eggs in her basket. Next spring, her babies will come out of them. Each one will begin to build his own basket. We can see the plan of **creation** in the lives of these little moths.

The Caddisworm

Many insects live an amazing life. One of these is the **caddisworm**. He has a funny little house. It is made of tiny shells and stones, or leftover parts of plants. The caddisworm has a very soft little body. He could not live long in the water without his house. A hungry fish would love to eat him!

The caddisworm needs a safe place to live. Jesus made him

in a special way. He can build his own home. He has to build it right in the water. He picks up little shells or bits of stone, or whatever he

Caddisworms in Different Cases

can find. He sticks them together with silk. He makes the silk himself. It works

like glue. It holds his home together.

The caddisworm begins his house when he is very little. As he grows bigger, he must keep adding to it. One day, he is ready to change. He puts a little silk door on the end of his house. He stays inside while his body changes. Soon he is no longer a worm. He grows wings. Then he is called a **caddisfly**.

Many flies and moths and butterflies have gone through a big change. It is called a **metamorphosis**.

They start as worms and become flying bugs. This is another miracle of God.

A Mosquito

Here is an enemy of ours. She has a graceful body, but none of us will ever like her. She is a pest! We do not like her bite.

Be on guard mosquito! We will fight back if you attack us. We do not enjoy the mosquito at all, but we can still learn something interesting about her. Knowing more about the mosquito can help us. We can find ways to keep her from living near our homes.

Mosquito Eggs

It rained a few days ago. Water filled an old bucket behind the shed. Something is **floating** in the water. What can it be? It is a whole boat of mosquito eggs glued together. It seems like a strange place for a mosquito to lay her eggs, but the babies will hatch in just the right spot.

Wigglers

After a while, little **wigglers** come out of these eggs. They wiggle as they swim through the water. How funny they are! They have little hairs at the end of their tails. They breathe through these hairs. As they grow larger, they split open their skins and come out. You can see their old skins floating on still water.

The Mosquitoes Grow Up

When mosquitoes first hatch, they are called **larvae**. Some people call them "wigglers." After a while, they begin to change. Their upper bodies and heads grow bigger. Now the babies do not eat. They are called **pupae**. Some people call them tumblers, because they move by rolling over and over.

Eggs

Adult

Larva

Pupa

Soon the mosquitoes break their skins and come out. They are full grown mosquitoes. They must be very careful while drying their wings. They will drown if they fall in the water. Their birth place is no longer safe for them.

Now the mosquitoes are ready to bite. Their bites can make us itch. Some mosquito bites can even make people sick. In parts of the world, mosquitoes carry **germs**. They can pass the germs to people through their bites.

You can help to keep mosquitoes away from your home. Do not leave buckets or cans to fill up with rainwater. The mosquitoes can not lay their eggs in your yard if there is no water.

The Housefly

The housefly is an insect. It has three body parts and six legs. The fly has sticky pads on its legs. That is why it can walk on the ceiling. The fly has large eyes. It can see on all sides. The fly has two wings. They fold flat against the fly's back when he is not using them.

The housefly is a pest. It does not bite us like the mosquito does. It carries germs on its body. When the fly lands, it leaves some of the germs behind. People can get sick from these germs. Stay out of my house, housefly!

Outside, the fly can do some good. It eats garbage and other things that make the air bad. Even a fly has its place in the world.

The Ichneumon Fly

The **ichneumon fly** has a long, hard name. It means, "a tracker." She is a wonderful **tracker**. No hunter or dog could find his food better.

The ichneumon fly hunts for **larvae**. These are the wormlike babies of other insects. She lays her eggs in or on the larvae. She has a sharp drill. She uses it to reach the larvae. Sometimes she has to drill into a tree to find the right place to lay her eggs. When the ichneumon fly's babies hatch, they use the larvae for food.

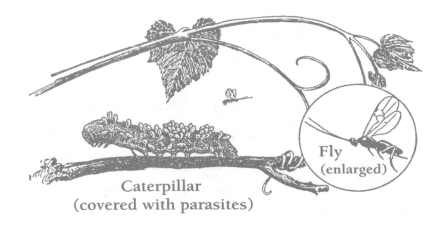

Caterpillar
(covered with parasites)

Fly
(enlarged)

The ichneumon fly is a good friend. Many of the worms that her babies eat are harmful pests. When the ichneumon fly's babies destroy larvae, they save many of our plants and trees from damage.

The Eagle

The bald eagle is a special bird because it stands for the United States. It has a brown body and a white head. From far away, it looks like the feathers are

missing from its head. That is why it is called "bald."

The eagle has a hooked beak. It has sharp, curved **claws**. Its wings and body are large and powerful.

The bald eagle is a sea eagle. Its home is near the water. Some eagles eat rabbits and birds. The main food of the bald eagle is fish. The eagle has very good eyesight. It can see small things as far as three miles away!

The eagle is a beautiful bird. It is good for man because it helps to control pests.

A Leaf-Cutter Bee

Not all bees live in hives. Some bees are solitary bees. They build a nest only for their own babies. They do not belong to a colony.

One solitary bee is a leaf cutter. She digs a tunnel under a rock or in a piece of wood. Sometimes her home is under a **shingle** on a roof. God has given this bee a special gift. She knows how to cut a circle! She cuts out pieces of leaves. She brings them to her tunnel. She lays them beside one another. She makes them into a bundle shaped like a tiny cup. She uses

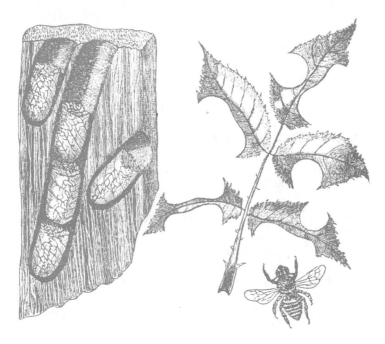

many, many circles of leaf. When she is finished, she lays her egg inside.

The **leaf-cutter bee** makes beebread from pollen. She leaves it in the nest with her egg. When the baby hatches, it will have food to eat until it grows up.

The Cuckoo Bee

Another solitary bee is called the **cuckoo bee**. She has a different way of caring for her babies. To us, it seems like she tries to trick the bumblebee. The mother cuckoo bee can do this because she looks very much like a bumblebee.

When she is ready to lay her eggs, she creeps into a bumblebee hive. She finds a cell that has been prepared by the worker bees. She lays her egg.

The bumblebees are often tricked. They do not know that the cuckoo bee has fooled them. They take care of her baby as if it were their own.

The cuckoo bee does not have to do a lot of work to care for her baby. She does make sure that it will have a home.

A Butterfly

What a beautiful butterfly! He darts around the yard. He is as pretty as the flowers on which he lands. He drinks nectar from the flowers.

The butterfly is an insect. He has two sets of wings.

They are joined by a hook. His wings are very delicate. Inside of them, there are **tubes** filled with air. If you touch a butterfly, you can damage his wings.

The butterfly was not always so nice to look at. When he hatched from his egg, he was a caterpillar. He crawled on trees and ate leaves. As he grew, his skin got too tight. The caterpillar split open his old skin and left it behind. He had a new skin all ready under the old one!

Soon he was ready for the big change. He wrapped himself in a tough skin called a **chrysalis**. After many weeks, he broke out. He was a butterfly! This change is called a **metamorphosis**. What a miracle! Only God could plan such a thing.

The Gallfly

What is this? It grew in an oak tree, but it is not an acorn. It is a little round house. It has no doors or windows. How can anything get in there? Nothing can get in very easily, but something will come out.

How do you suppose something got in the house? It grew in there! Its house grew, too. Is that not strange?

The creature in the house is a baby **gallfly**. His mother put him in the oak

tree. She drilled a hole in the bark. She put an egg in the hole. She also put in something very special. It was a **chemical** which caused a gall to grow. The gall is her baby's house.

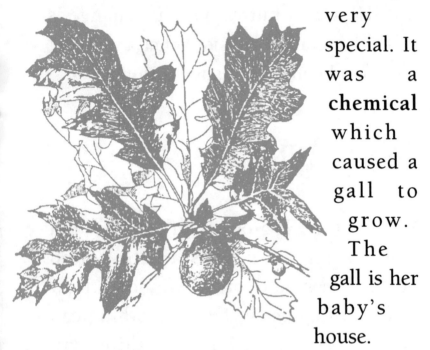

The Gallfly Hatches

The baby gallfly hatches from his egg. He is still inside the **gall**. He will begin at once to eat his house. It seems strange, but it is just what he needs for food. How handy for him!

The gallfly does not have to come out of his house to find food. He eats and eats. Finally, he has eaten enough. He goes to sleep. While he is asleep, he turns into a gallfly like his mother. He is ready to go out into the world.

The gall does not have a door. This does not matter to the gallfly. He knows what to do. He cuts his way through the wall of his house, and flies away. He is done with his house now.

The Gall

The gallfly's little, round house was the perfect place for him to grow. The **gall** gave him food and a place to live. The gall can also be useful to people. We can not eat it, or live in it, but we can make something useful from it.

The Gall—showing the larva in its cell

There is a **chemical** in the gall that can be used to make good, black ink. How odd to think that the home of an insect could be used like that! The great Creator God has made the animals perform in a wonderful way for the good of man.

The Grasshopper

The grasshopper is an insect with long, strong legs. He can jump very far. Many grasshoppers have wings as well. When the grasshopper sits still, you cannot see his wings. They are folded up like a fan. Long, straight covers keep the wings safe.

When the grasshopper flies, you can see what big, fine wings he has. They are nearly as pretty as a butterfly's wings.

In other ways, the grasshopper is not like the butterfly. When a grasshopper hatches from its egg, it is not a crawling worm. It looks like a tiny, adult grasshopper. The baby does not have any wings. When the baby grows bigger, his outside gets too small. Soon, he splits down the back and

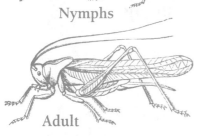

Nymphs

Adult

steps out of his outside skin. His new skin is all ready under the old one. This is called **molting**. Most grasshoppers molt five times. With each molting, the grasshopper's wings get bigger. When the grasshopper becomes an adult, his wings are fully grown.

The grasshopper is food for many birds, **toads**, and **lizards**. In some countries, even the people eat grasshoppers!

Grasshoppers can be very greedy. Sometimes a lot of them can eat a farmer's whole crop. In the Bible, God used one kind of grasshopper as a curse. The insects ate all of the Egyptians' crops when their **Pharaoh** refused to obey Him. God can use even the smallest, or weakest, of creatures to do His will.

Asleep in the Ground

In the winter, the earth is hard and bare. There are no ants crawling on the ground. No grasshoppers fly away when we brush by the tall, brown grasses. Very few living things greet us, as they did in the summer.

What has happened to all of the tiny creatures? Most of them are not dead. They are hidden away. The ants are down in their home in the ground. They have stored food down there for the long, cold months. The frogs have hidden in the mud, to sleep all winter. Many caterpillars sleep in their **cocoons**, slowly changing into their adult forms. Some spiders have hidden inside of dead leaves on the ground. Crickets and grasshoppers have left their eggs in the ground. Here and there, under logs and stones or in cracks, wasps and bumblebees and other creatures have hidden. In their hives, the honey bees spend their winter. They have plenty of sweet honey to eat.

As we go about in this cold, winter weather, it seems as if nearly all life is gone. It only sleeps, though, in **bud** and **seed**, in egg and cocoon, in earth and in water.

The Spirit of God, the Giver of Life, will wake up all these creatures in the spring.

Wake Up!

It is spring. The gentle south wind has come again. The cold north wind will stop. It has played rough games long enough. There will be no more ice and snow. The spring sun and gentle rains have begun.

Many insects and animals have been asleep in their snug houses all winter. The spring weather will wake them up. The sun warms the earth and air. The rain taps gently on the tiny creatures' doors. The south wind calls softly, "Wake up! Your long winter sleep is over."

The little ants can begin their work now. The frogs can creep out of their mud houses. The flowers will make pollen for the bees to eat. The flowers need the bees as well, to help them make their seeds. The butterflies and moths are ready to break out of their cocoons.

Animals and insects are eager for the spring. The winter has been long and cold. The spring brings new life. The world is a busy, buzzing, working, living place now. God's little creatures are happy to do their jobs. We can learn a lot about hard work from the ants and bees!

The Prairie

A **prairie** is a wide, flat place. For miles there are no hills or trees. Many of the plants on a prairie are tall grasses.

The grasses give food for many animals. **Bison** and **antelope** graze on the plains. These animals travel together in herds. They eat the grasses, and then move on to find water or more food.

Jesus has made a place to fit the needs of every living thing. The plants on the prairie support many creatures, large and small.

Prairie Life

Large animals like bison and antelopes are easy to see as they graze on the plains. Other, smaller creatures are not so easy to see.

Prairie dogs, gophers, rabbits and mice live in holes, or **burrows** in the ground. The prairie dog and the rabbit come out of their holes to eat plants. The **pocket gopher** digs around under the ground. He gathers grass roots in his pockets. The pockets are slits on the outside of his cheeks. When he has filled his pockets, he brings the roots to his **storeroom**. He pushes the food out of his cheeks in the same way that you push toothpaste out of the tube!

The prairie may look still to us sometimes. That is because many of the animals which live there are under the ground!

Prairie Hunters

Some animals on the prairie like to eat meat. These hunters catch plant-eating animals for their food.

Prairie creatures have ways to protect themselves from the hunters. The little animals are able to hide in the ground. Their coats blend in with the earth and grasses, making them hard to see. Larger animals, like antelopes, get away from danger by running very fast.

Far above the prairie, **hawks** fly high on the winds. God has given them very good eyesight. When they see the movement of a rabbit or a prairie dog, they dive towards the earth. They catch

their **prey** with their strong, sharp feet, called **talons**.

The hunters serve a purpose on the prairie. They help to keep down the number of smaller creatures. Too many rabbits and gophers could damage the prairie plants, then the other animals would not have enough food.

A Coyote Trick

The **coyote** is another prairie hunter. He is not always quick enough to catch the fast antelope. Several coyotes work together, and use a clever trick to catch their prey.

One trick is a like a relay race. The prize is an antelope! The coyotes choose one animal out of the herd. Then, three or four coyotes run out into the plain and hide in the grasses.

The first coyote runs up and chases the antelope that was chosen. The antelope is much faster, and easily gets away. The coyotes have a plan. The first coyote chases the antelope toward the second coyote, hidden in the grasses. The second coyote jumps up, and chases the antelope toward the third coyote.

Each coyote has run for only a little way. The antelope has run for miles. Soon he is tired. One by one, the coyotes catch up to him. Together, they enjoy their prize.

An Owl

One day, a boy and his father went hunting. The boy sat down on a log to rest. After a moment, his father came up.

"Son," he said, "Do you see the owl?"

"Where?" said the boy.

"Beside you on the log," said his father.

The owl sat almost near enough for the boy to touch it, but he had not seen it. Do you know why? The owl was sitting very still. He did not move. His feathers were nearly the same color as the log, so that he looked like a part of it. He did not open his big eyes. He only peeped through one eye to see what the boy was doing. The owl did not get scared and jump off the log. He seemed to think that if he sat very still, the boy would not

see him. This seems like a funny idea, but it was his way of protecting himself. When an animal hides by becoming like the plants and ground where he lives, it is called **camouflage**. It is like wearing special clothes. God made many creatures in this way to protect them from their enemies.

A Beaver and a Squirrel

"Good morning little squirrel; may I ask what you are doing?" said a beaver.

"Yes," said the squirrel. "I am working very hard to lay up my winter store of nuts."

"How do you get those nuts cracked?" asked the beaver. "You are so little, I can't believe you can do it!"

"Yes, I can," said the squirrel. "I do it with my sharp teeth. Watch me as I turn a nut over in my sharp claws and **gnaw** on it. My teeth

wear away as I use them. That keeps them sharp. They keep growing all the time, so that they do not wear out."

"My teeth are like that, too!" said the beaver. "But I can gnaw much bigger things than nuts with my teeth. I can gnaw down a tree."

"Really?" said the squirrel. "But why would you want to do that?"

"Beavers need trees to make a **dam** across the water," said the beaver. "Many of us work together in the winter. We work better as a team."

A Beaver Dam

"How do you make your houses?" the squirrel asked.

"Beavers make houses out of sticks covered over with mud," said the beaver.

"How do you cover them? asked the squirrel.

"We do it with our tails. They are our **trowels**." said the beaver.

"Is that why you have such strange, flat tails?" asked the squirrel.

"Yes, it is. We could not work very well if we had such long,

hairy tails as yours. Your tail is beautiful, but I do not think it does you any good," said the beaver.

"You are wrong!" said the squirrel. "My tail is so light that it bears me up when I leap from one part of the tree to another."

"I must tell you more about what we can build," said the beaver. "We like to have the water come up over our front door. We are safer then. Sometimes the water does not come up high enough. We have to build a **dam** to make it rise higher. We cut down all the trees we need. We build a dam of trees and sticks and stones, and cover it with mud. Our dam holds back the water. The pond gets deep enough to cover our door."

"How do you get into your house if the water comes over the front door?" asked the squirrel.

"We swim into it. Our hind feet are **webbed**, so they make good paddles for swimming," said the beaver. "I see that your feet are not like mine. You have sharp claws. What are they for?"

"My claws help me to cling to the tree as I climb up," said the squirrel.

"We are not much alike," said the beaver.

"No," said the squirrel, "But we are both perfectly made to do our jobs."

The Duck and the Hen

"Good morning, hen," quacked the duck.

"Good morning," clucked the hen.

"Let's take a walk," said the duck.

"Very well, duck, I would be glad to go with you. I enjoy taking a walk. I always find so many good things to eat on the way."

"Let's go down to the pond and have a swim," said the duck.

"Swim!" said the hen. "Not I! My feathers would get so wet and messy. I even run in out of the rain if I can. I look like a fright when I get wet. It makes me angry, too. No, no, you will not catch me going into the water."

"That is strange," said the duck. "I love to go into the water all the time. My feathers do not even get wet. Water slips right off of my back. You may not be able to swim, hen, but you can run much faster than I can. The children laugh when they see me running. They say that I **waddle**. That is because my legs are set so far back on my body. It is easier to swim with legs like that."

"Oh, duck, let's stop here and scratch a bit! I'm sure we can find a nice lunch," said the hen.

"Well, now, that is something I cannot do," said the duck. "Look at my feet! Do you see the web between my toes? No, I cannot scratch. I'll just take a dip in the pond. I will put my broad, flat bill down into the mud to find my lunch."

"I am afraid my sharp bill would do very little good in the mud," said the hen. "I'll just scratch here until you come back. We can walk home together."

The Best Coat

The coats of many creatures are very different from each other. Which creature has the best coat?

A fish has hard, shiny **scales**. Each scale covers some of the next scale to keep the water out. The scales are hard so that they cannot soak up water. Water would make them heavy. They are oily so that the fish can slip easily through the water.

They are in many pieces so that he can bend easily when he swims. Could he have a better coat?

The Bird's Coat

A bird looks very different from a fish. It has a beautiful coat, all made of feathers. How soft and light they are! They are not heavy for the bird to carry as she flies. In fact, she needs her feathers to fly. She spreads out her wings. Her feathers open wide. She can push against a lot of air with them. This helps her to rise. The bird has a wonderful coat!

An Oyster's Coat

It is amazing how God has made each animal in a different way. An oyster does not look like a fish or a bird. His coat is very thick and hard. It is made from two pieces.

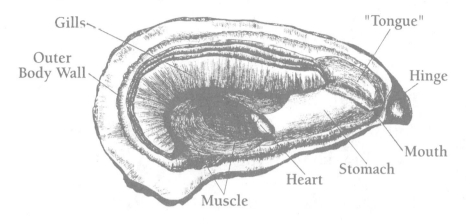

Gills
Outer Body Wall
"Tongue"
Hinge
Mouth
Stomach
Heart
Muscle

It can open like a book. The oyster lives inside a hard **shell** so he can be safe.

How can the oyster move with such a heavy coat? He does not need to move! An oyster lives in the water. He eats tiny pieces of food that float in the water. He pulls the water into his shell. His food is in the water. He will stay in the same spot, on a shell or a rock, for his whole life.

The oyster's coat is so hard because his body is so soft. He needs a hard cover to keep him from harm. The oyster's shell is perfect for him.

The Bear's Coat

The black bear lives in the mountains and forests of North America. He has a great big, shaggy **fur** coat.

The bear eats roots, seeds, fruit and insects. Sometimes he eats fish or larger animals. One of his favorite treats, though, is honey.

When a bear finds a bees' nest, he tears it up with his claws. He laps up all the sweet honey he can find. His thick, long fur protects him from the bees. The only place they can sting him is on his nose! The bear's fur is a wonderful coat.

What if a bird had scales? Could it fly? Could a fish swim if it had a hard shell? What would an oyster do with a fur coat? Would feathers protect a bear from bee stings?

Our wise Creator made each animal with the very best coat for him.

A Cuttlefish

A big fish was swimming about in the sea, looking for food. Soon, he saw a **cuttlefish**. "Now I shall have a good dinner," thought the big fish. He swam after the cuttlefish as fast as he could.

 The little fish swam quickly, also.

Suddenly, the water ahead of the big fish became black. "What happened?" thought the big fish. "I cannot see anything! Has it become night, or have I gone blind? Most important of all, where is my dinner?"

The big fish swam around as best as he could. Soon, he came to clear water again. It was as light and as bright as before. What had become of the cuttlefish? The cuttlefish carries an ink bag with him. When he saw that the big fish was about to catch him, he emptied his bag into the water. It made the water black all around him. The big fish could not see him. The cuttlefish could easily swim away! What a clever way to save himself from danger!

A Cocoon

Here is a **cocoon**. It is built around a little brown twig. We cannot see inside of it. It does not make any noise. It seems like a poor, dead thing. What is going on inside this little brown house?

A caterpillar made this cocoon. He used to live in a maple tree. He ate the leaves until he grew big and fat.

One day, he began to spin. He spun and worked until his house was done. He made the brown walls thick and warm. The cold does not bother him. He will sleep inside his cocoon until he has made a big change.

The Moth

A caterpillar slept in a brown cocoon. When a hole appeared in the side of the cocoon, it was not a caterpillar that crept out. It was a **moth**!

How did the moth get into the cocoon? Where did the caterpillar go? The moth was the caterpillar! She went through a big change. The change is called **metamorphosis**. It is a miracle.

The moth stretched her **wrinkled** wings. Soon they were straight and strong. They looked like soft, furry skin. Her **feelers** looked like little **ferns**. She was a much prettier creature than the worm she used to be.

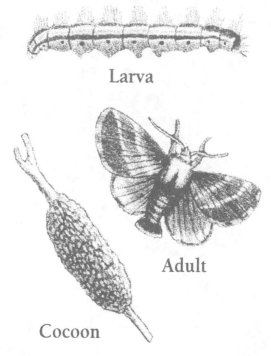

Larva

Adult

Cocoon

The moth flew away. Soon, she laid some eggs on a maple leaf. Tiny caterpillars hatched out. One day, they would fly instead of crawling, too.

The Kingbird

The **kingbird** sits high on a treetop. From his **perch**, he can look everywhere. He is watching for other birds. He will fight them if he must.

Why would the kingbird want to fight? Is he mean? No, he has a very good reason for fighting. He and his mate made a nest in a cherry tree. The **female** is sitting in the nest now.

The **male** is sitting high above. He sits there all day. He will protect his little mate. If another bird comes, he gives a **shrill** cry. He flies after the other bird.

The other day a **woodpecker** came to eat the cherries. The kingbird does not eat cherries. He eats insects. Even so, he would not allow the woodpecker to come near. The kingbird did not want the woodpecker to bother his mate. He flew after him. He pulled out some of his feathers! The woodpecker was glad to get away.

The kingbird is brave. He never leaves his post. Even a **thundershower** does not bother him. He just sits there, even if he does get wet.

His mate does her part, sitting on the eggs. Soon, the kingbirds will have a house full of children.

The Robin

"Cheer up, cheer up—cheer, cheer!"

The pretty robin sings a sweet song. He is not a fighter like the kingbird. Still, he does know how to protect his mate.

When the robin's nest is built, the male moves to a tree nearby. His bright, orange breast is easy to see. He sings his cheery song.

His mate can hear him sing. She sits for

hours on her eggs. His song keeps her from getting lonely. The female robin does not have a orange breast. She does not sing on the treetops. Her brown coat is the same color as her nest and the tree limbs. It would be hard for a cat, or some other creature to see her.

The male robin keeps his mate safe by making others watch him—not her.

The Ant

Have you ever watched an ant at work? The worker ant is a busy creature. He is part of a **colony**. The ants in a colony work together. They gather food. They care for the queen and her babies.

There are many kinds of ants. Ants are insects. They have six legs. They have three body parts and two **antennae**. Ants use their antennae to touch and to smell things. When an ant finds food, he lays

down a trail of **scent** back to his nest. Now other ants can follow the trail. Each ant can carry only a tiny bit of food. Together, many ants carry enough food for the whole colony.

The Life of an Ant

Each year, many new queen ants fly off to start new colonies. An ant can fly? Yes, the queen ant has wings! When she finds a home she does not need to fly anymore. She takes her wings off!

The queen ant lays many eggs. Larvae hatch out of the eggs. The queen ant cares for her babies. Soon, the larvae spin cocoons. In the pupa stage,  they change into worker ants.

Egg   Larva   Pupa Stage

When the worker ants come out of their cocoons, they are ready to help the queen. They take care of the eggs and larvae. They dig tunnels and search for food. A busy new ant colony has begun.

Honey Ants

Ants are the same in some ways. In other ways, ants can be very different from each other. One special kind of ant is called a **honey ant**. The honey ants love sweets.

Some honey ant workers are called **repletes**.

The repletes live in a special room. Other workers bring them nectar and honeydew. The repletes eat and eat. They become huge. They cannot even move! They hang from the ceiling in their room. Other workers can come to them for food. The repletes are like living honey pots.

When the **weather** is cold or dry, the ants can still have sweet food.

More About Honey Ants

Honey ants feed nectar and **honeydew** to the repletes. They store the sweet food in their bodies. The honey ants gather the nectar from flowers, but where do they get the honeydew? They gather it from insects called **aphids**. Honey ants take care of their own herds. Their herds are not cows. They are aphids.

Aphids live on plants. They suck the juices from the **stems** and **roots**. Then, they make honeydew. The ants get the honeydew by gently rubbing the backs of the aphids with their **antennae**.

The ants take care of their  herd of aphids. They protect them from their enemies. They keep the aphids out of the bad weather. They care for the aphids' eggs. They even carry the aphids from one plant to another when they need more food.

People do not like aphids. Aphids destroy plants like cotton and sugar cane. Farmers are happy when birds and ladybugs eat the aphids. The ants are not happy to lose their herd.

The Fungus-Growing Ant

Another special ant is called the **fungus-growing** ant. The worker ants in these colonies grow their own little gardens.

Fungus ants gather leaves. They carry the leaves over their heads like **umbrellas**. They find a special place to grow their garden. The ants chew the leaves into **pulp**. The pulp is a perfect place for fungus to grow. Soon the ants have a beautiful garden. They can gather their food very easily.

Did you know that ants could grow a garden? God made them very wisely, did He not?

The Best Jumper

"I can jump farther than you."

"No, you can't. I can jump the farthest."

Did you ever hear children talk like that? If a child tried very hard, he might be able to jump six feet. That would be less than two times his own length.

Do you know what is one of the best jumpers? It is the **flea**. He is an odd looking insect. He has

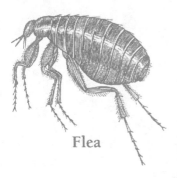

Flea

very strong legs. His body is covered with plates of hard, tough skin. The flea can be harmful to animals and to people. Still, it is interesting to learn about him.

There is one thing he can do better than anyone else. He can jump two hundred times his own length! His long hind legs help him to do it. What a spring he must make to go so far!

If a child could jump like that, he could go more than eight hundred feet at one leap! That would be fun!

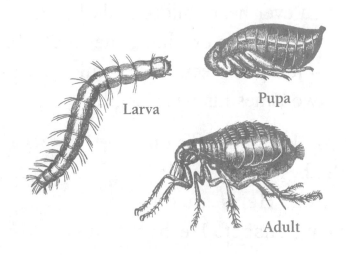

Larva

Pupa

Adult

The Mayfly

The little **mayfly** is a beautiful insect. Sometimes she is called a "dayfly." That is because she has only one day to enjoy her beautiful wings.

The mayfly spent most of her life as a **nymph**. She came out of an egg which her mother left on the top of the water. For two or three years,

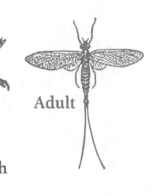

Adult

Nymph

she swam in a pond. Her wings grew while she lived in the water. They were kept shut up in a tight case. She was getting ready for one, beautiful day in the air.

When she was ready, she crept out of the water, and out of her old skin. Now she is a dainty and pretty creature. Her insides are full of air. She can not even eat!

The mayfly does not need to live more than a day. She has only one thing to do; she must lay her eggs on the water. Her life's work is quickly done.

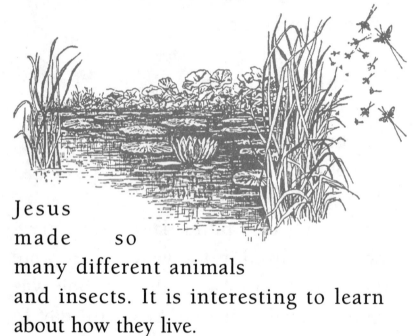

Jesus made so many different animals and insects. It is interesting to learn about how they live.

Tumblebugs

Two big **beetles** are rolling a ball. What are they doing? Are they playing a game? They roll, push and tug the ball with all of their might. The beetles are not playing. They are working very hard.

They have come to a hill. How can they get up? Push and tug! Push and tug! They are almost to the top! Oh, no! A slip—and down they go, bugs and ball to the foot of the hill. It looks very funny.

Do they give up their task? No! They get up and try again.

Finally they reach the top of the hill. Down they go, rolling over and over, on the other side. The beetles get up again and continue their task.

What does this mean? Where did the beetles get the ball? What are they going to do with it?

The beetles made the ball themselves. It has an egg inside of it. The ball is made of food for the baby to eat when it has hatched. The beetles are going to take the ball to a safe place. They will cover it up, and their baby will be safe.

Boys and girls can learn a lesson from the beetles. Do not give up just because a job is hard. Keep working, and you will get your job done.

A Little Carpenter

A little **carpenter bee** flies around the branches of a maple tree. She is very busy. She is building her house.

How can a bee build a house from a tree? Does she saw the branches down? Does she have a hammer and nails to put the sticks together?

No!

The bee has special tools that God gave to her. She does not have to carry away the wood to make her home. She drills right

into a twig. She makes a hole in the tiny branch. She makes a round front room. Down the middle of the twig, she makes more rooms. She builds walls between the rooms. She uses the chippings made from the drilling of the twig. She has a special glue that she makes herself. She sticks the chips together to make each wall. Each room will be the home for a new baby bee.

Carpenter bees can not try new ways to build houses, like people can. You will not find a carpenter bee making a castle, or an apartment building in her tree. She does what God made her to do. She builds a perfect home for her family.

The Walking Stick

God has made so many different kinds of insects. Some of them seem very strange to us. One odd looking insect is the **walking stick**. His name tells what he is like. He looks almost like a stick or twig. When he walks, he looks just like his name—a walking stick!

Why do you think he looks the way he does? God made him that way to protect him. The walking stick can sit very still in a bush or a tree. His shape and color match the twigs. His strange looks protect him. Birds and other creatures like to eat insects. Since they think that the walking stick is a twig, they leave him alone.

God knew the best way to make every creature. We can remember this when we see the walking stick.

A Ladybug

The ladybug is a pretty little insect. Some people call her a "ladybird beetle." She has a red or orange back with black spots. Her brightly colored back protects her delicate wings. When she wants to fly, she folds her wing covers out of the way.

The ladybug knows how to protect herself. She can not fight her enemies, but she can fool them. When she is scared, she drops down to the ground. She curls up her legs and lays very still. Many creatures will leave her alone if they think she is dead.

Some ladybirds have a different way of protecting themselves. When this kind of ladybug is scared, she gives off a bad smell. Her enemy does not want to be near her. He does not want to eat something that smells like that! The enemy goes away. The ladybird beetle is safe.

Our Friend the Ladybug

The ladybug is not just a pretty insect. She is our friend. She never bites or bothers people. In fact, she is very helpful to us.

Tiny green bugs called **aphids** sometimes live on plants. They eat the leaves and make the plants sick. Farmers do not like these bugs. They make it hard to grow crops.

These little green bugs are the ladybug's favorite food! She eats as many of them as she can. She saves the plants. She helps the farmer grow the food that we eat.

The Ladybug's Children

The ladybug eats harmful insects. When she is ready, she lays her eggs. Her children do not look like her when they hatch. They are dark-colored **grubs** with yellow spots. Her little ones are like her in one way. The ladybug's babies like to eat the same kind of food that she does.

The grubs grow very fast. They need a lot of food. The greedy worms eat a lot of harmful bugs.

Later, the grubs go to sleep in cases glued to the bottom side of leaves. When they come out of the cases, they will be adult ladybugs.

Pupa

Adults

Larva (Grub)

Ladybugs are so helpful that people sometimes gather them in the winter, when they **hibernate**. The farmers keep the ladybugs in a cold place. Then, when their crops are ready, they spread the ladybugs on their fields. What an important insect the ladybug is!

A Little Actor

One day, a little girl walked in the **meadow**. She saw a little **quail** fluttering along in front of her. She could not see where it came from.

"Poor little thing," she said. "How lame you are! You must be badly hurt. I will pick you up and see what I can do for you."

But the little girl could not pick up the quail. Just as she reached for the bird, it flew away as well as could be.

Why did the quail act like it was hurt? It was because the quail was a mother. When she saw the girl coming near, she was afraid her babies could be hurt. She began to limp and flutter away from her nest. When she got far enough away from her little ones, she flew away. What

a clever mother! She works hard
protect her little ones.

The little girl was so busy watching the
mother quail, she never saw the nest.
The quail uses the same trick to fool wild
animals that might harm her babies.
Jesus made her very wise.

Gymnast

The **looper** is a funny little caterpillar. He makes his body into a loop as he walks. Do you know why he walks that way? He has no legs in the middle part of his body. He moves by walking his back legs up to his front legs, and then moving his front legs as far as his body can stretch.

When Mr. Looper walks, it looks like he is measuring. He uses his own body as a ruler. That is why he is often called an **inchworm**.

Have you ever seen an inchworm hanging in the air? He has spun a silken thread. He

Mr. Looper (hanging by his thread)

can lower himself to the ground. He can also climb back up his thread.

Mr. Looper has another trick. He can hold himself to a twig using only his back legs. He can stretch his body straight out. It must be hard work! He looks almost exactly like a twig when he does it. Can you imagine why he would do that? Maybe the birds will think he is only a twig, and will leave him alone. Is it not wonderful that even a measuring worm has a way to protect himself?

A Living Light

This little bug flies around at night. He does not mind the dark. Why should he?

He carries his own little light with him. Have you ever seen him with his little candle? You call him a **firefly**, or a "lightning bug."

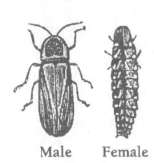

Male   Female

His light is not like fire. It does not burn him. It will not feel warm to you if you hold your hand near him. Still, he makes a bright light! They turn their lights on and off as they fly. How beautiful it looks to see these little bugs flying about at night!

The firefly has a very plain body during the day. We would hardly see him among so many bright-colored flowers and butterflies. At night we cannot see the flowers and butterflies. We can see the firefly, as he does his part to make the world bright.

A Little Messenger

This little bee is a faithful **messenger**, but he does not work for the post office. He is busy carrying tiny packages in the fields on hot summer days.

What can such a tiny creature carry? Can it be of any use? Yes! This bee carries dust. It is not normal dust. It is flower dust, or **pollen**, from the red clover. When the bee flies from one red clover to another, the dust clings to him. Then the dust is rubbed off on another flower. If the bee did not carry the dust from one flower to another, the clover could not make seeds. There would be no new clover. Red clover is an important crop for some farmers. The tiny bee turns out to be important to people!

Why does the bee do this job for the flowers? He does not know that he is helping the clover. He is working hard to get **nectar**. His colony can use it to make sweet honey. Is it not wonderful that God made His creation to care for itself so well?

A Little Gardener

The **earthworm** is a small, helpless creature. He is not pretty to look at. He has no eyes and no legs. It is even hard to tell which end of him is his head! It does not seem like such a simple animal could be of any use.

In truth, the earthworm is very useful to man. The earthworm is a gardener! He does not have a shovel or a wagon to carry dirt. Instead, he uses his own body to move the soil! He eats the dirt. He crawls to the top of the ground and leaves the dirt there. While the dirt is in the worm's body, it becomes richer. The soil which a worm has carried is better for growing crops.

The holes where the worm crawls are also useful. They help the rainwater to drain into the soil.

One worm can not do a lot of good. Thousands of earthworms together, though, are a great help to the soil. Each worm does his part, and the farmer's fields are made richer.

A Hummingbird

The tiny **hummingbird** is a beautiful creature. It is amazing to see her fly. Her wings move so quickly, they can hardly be seen. She can **hover**, which means she can fly in one spot, as if she were floating! The hummingbird can even fly backwards, or upside down!

The hummingbird's beautiful feathers match the pretty flowers. It is hard to see her as she hovers above the **blossoms**. She puts her long beak into a flower, and laps up nectar and insects.

The hummingbird's nest is made from leafy bits, and is sometimes held together by spiders' webs. The nest is so small, it looks like a knot on the limb of a tree.

The hummingbird is so small and light, it can become caught on a **thistle**! Some insects and frogs can catch and eat these tiny birds.

Hummingbirds like to drink from tube feeders filled with sugar water. People hang these feeders in their yards. It is so interesting to watch hummingbirds fly!

A Hawkmoth

What is this flying over the flowers? Is it a hummingbird? It looks a little like one.

When it stops, we can see that this creature is not a bird. It is an insect, called a **hawkmoth**. It has six legs and four wings, instead of two legs and two wings. It has no beak like a bird.

The hawkmoth has a very long tongue, like a hair.

He can unroll it until it is several inches long. He uses it to reach down into the flowers that have long tubes. He is as dainty about his food as is a hummingbird.

The hawkmoth was not always so dainty. He began life on a tomato vine. So, he was named a **tomato worm**. He was very greedy. He had a strange way of raising his head.

When the tomato worm was ready, he went down into the ground. He did not need to make a thick cocoon to keep him warm in the winter. The earth kept him warm. He slept inside a little case. There was a long stem on one side of the case. Maybe his long tongue was stored there.

When spring came, he crept out of his dark bed. He came out to feed upon the flowers. The tomato worm is such an plain creature. What a miracle that God made him to fly one day!

A Snail

Some creatures, like the hummingbird, move so fast you can hardly see them. Others, like the **snail**, are so slow, they barely seem to move.

Why is a snail so slow? He has only one foot with which to creep along. Also, he has to carry his house along with him every place he goes!

Why does the snail not leave his home? Could he not move more quickly if he did not have to carry his heavy **shell**? Maybe he could move more quickly, but he would not

be safe without his shell. The snail's body is very soft. The shell protects his delicate skin. It also saves him from being eaten by a bird or some other creature.

Since the snail carries his house on his back, he does not have to be fast. If there is danger, he just pulls up inside his shell.

Carrying his home, the snail is able to go where he needs to go. It really does not matter if it takes him a long time.

A Dragonfly

The **dragonfly** has four beautiful wings. He has big, bright eyes. He is a large insect. He may seem a little scary, but we do not have to be afraid of him. He does

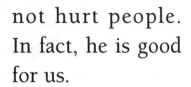

not hurt people. In fact, he is good for us.

The dragonfly eats insects. He likes to catch mosquitoes for his dinner. He can grab them as he flies. He holds them with his legs, and crushes them with his jaws. He can dart down very quickly. He eats a lot of insects because he is so big. Dragonflies can help to keep mosquitoes from bothering animals and people.

The Dragonfly's First Home

The dragonfly often finds his dinner near a pond. There are many insects near the water. Before the dragonfly had wings, he even lived in the water.

Dragonflies drop their eggs in a pond or lake. When an egg hatches, a **nymph** is born. The nymph swims in the water for a year or so. It uses its strong mouth to

catch insects. As the nymph swims, two pairs of wings grow under its skin.

One day, the nymph creeps out of the water. It sits on the stem of a water plant. Its old skin splits, and the dragonfly creeps out. He waits for his wings to spread out and grow strong.

Soon the dragonfly can fly quickly through the air. He darts here and there and catches mosquitoes. We will not miss the mosquitoes!

A Careful Mother

This insect mother is very different. Some people do no like her at all. She is not pretty to look at, and she does not have a pretty name, either. She is called an **earwig**. She likes to hide in dark, wet places; sometimes under a stone.

The earwig has strange little wings. They fold up like a fan. She crosses one on top of the other behind her back and puts them under her wing cases.

The earwig is different than a lot of insect mothers. We have read about bees and mayflies, who never see their own babies. The earwig does more than see her babies. She sits on her eggs like a mother hen! When the little ones hatch out, she leads them around to find food. She takes very good care of them.

Is it not strange that there are so many different ways these little creatures have of

caring for their children? There is always something new and interesting to learn about them. We could never learn all there is to know about God's wonderful creation.

God's Tiny Creatures

God's world is full of so many different kinds of creatures. We have learned that even the tiniest insect or worm lives his life just as Jesus made him to do.

We have learned about the amazing **skills** that God has given to many of his creatures. Some new babies know how to care for themselves at once. Many know how to build their own houses. Each one knows exactly what kind of food it needs. It knows where to find food, and how to get it.

Some creatures know how to spin a cocoon. They do it just in time to fall asleep. When they wake up, they have grown up like their parents.

Insects and other tiny creatures follow the same ways of their parents. They are born the same way. They go through the same changes. They build the same kinds of houses, and no better. They gather and eat the same kinds of food. They have been given the same kinds of tools. They use them in the same way that their parents did. They run or fly or crawl or walk in the same way that their parents did. We can see the plan of creation in the lives of the tiniest creatures.

The Most Wonderful Creature of All

Do you know what kind of baby is the most wonderful of all? He cannot take care of himself, like some babies can. He cannot make his own clothes or find his own food. He does not know how to build a house.

This baby's parents do all of these things for him. He cannot fly or swim or run. He cannot even walk or crawl until he is older and can learn how.

Do you know what kind of baby this is? He is a **human**, like you! He is not wonderful because of what he can do now. His **worth** is not in the things he will learn later, either. A person is the most wonderful creature because he is made in God's **image**. A person has a **soul** that will never die.

What Man Can Do

A newborn human is helpless. When he is grown, though, he is able to do wonderful things.

A man cannot run very fast, but he can make cars and trains. These can carry him much faster than any animal can run.

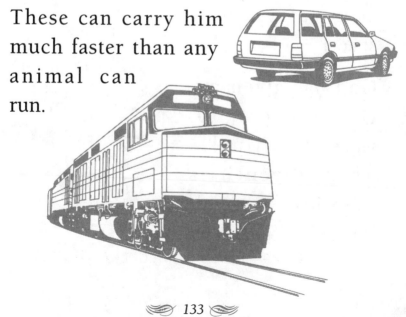

He cannot
swim very quickly,
but he can make a boat that
will carry him over the water faster than
a fish can swim. He can make a
submarine, so that he can travel
deep into the water as well.

A man cannot fly; but he
can make an airplane that
will carry him around the
world. **Rocket ships** can
even carry a man into
space!

God has given man
the **wisdom** to
invent things.
These **inventions**
help him to do things
more quickly and easily.

Man has no house given to him as the snail does, but he can learn to make a house. He is not born with feathers or scales or fur; but he can make beautiful clothes for himself. Man does not have to make his home or his clothes in exactly the same way that his parents did. He is free to try new and different plans.

A man does not have a light like a firefly, but he knows how to make light with **electricity**. He was not born with a saw or chisel like a beaver, or a drill like the carpenter bee; but he knows how to make many tools for himself.

Man was created in the image of God. That is why he can do such wonderful and amazing things. God made people to rule over the animals and to care for the earth.

Man's Inventions

Birds and bears, ants and bees: each has a special place in the world. Each creature can use the tools God has given it to live just the way God planned.

Man's special skill of **invention** allows him to change the way he lives.

Man can make a special glass called a **microscope**. It makes things look much larger than their real size. This allows man to learn about things that he could not even see with his own eyes.

Another special glass, the **telescope**, lets man see things that are far away, like the moon, the **planets** and the stars. Since they seem nearer, he can learn more about them with a telescope.

Man has the **telephone** to carry sound. He can hear sounds from the other side of the world with this invention.

The **television** lets man see pictures of things, as they happen, anywhere in the world. **Computers** help people to share helpful things with each other.

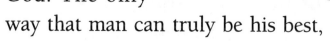

Man is a very wise and wonderful being. All of his special skills are gifts from God. The only way that man can truly be his best,

is if he fears God and keeps His **commandments**. Man is only wise when he follows the rules that God has given him for living.

Our Creator and Savior

The Bible tells us that God created the heaven and the earth in six days. On the fifth day, God made all the creatures of the sea and the birds of the air. On the sixth day, He made all the other animals that move over the earth.

On the sixth day, God also created man in His **image** and said that man should rule over the fish, birds, and animals—over all the earth. After God created Adam and Eve, He put them in a beautiful garden. Many of the same animals that you learned about in this book were probably living in the garden.

At this time, God made an agreement called a **covenant** with Adam. God commanded that Adam may freely eat from any tree in the garden, but not from the tree of knowledge of good and evil. If he obeyed God he would live, but if he broke God's law he would surely die.

Adam disobeyed God and **sin** entered the world. Satan tempted Eve first, then he used her to tempt Adam. They were no longer happy and tried to hide from God. Adam felt ashamed and even blamed Eve for what he had done.

The Bible says we are sinners, too. We are like the tumblebugs. Their eggs are put in a ball of dirt, which is like sin. When they hatch, the young start eating the ball of dirt. This reminds us that we also are born in sin and our hearts are dirty in every way.

God wants His children to be like the caterpillar that changes into a beautiful butterfly. When God calls us to be His children, the **Holy Spirit** gives us a new life. We are changed into a new creature because **Jesus Christ** died on the cross for our sins. "Therefore if any man be in Christ, he is a new creature: old things are passed away; behold, all things are become new" (2 Corinthians 5:17).

The greatest act of creation is when God changes a son or daughter, mom or dad, into a new creature. How do you become a new creature? Jesus said, "… Ye must be born again" (John 3:7). This means God needs to change you, just like He changes the caterpillar into a butterfly. Everything becomes new!

"For whosoever shall call upon the name of the Lord shall be saved" (Romans 10:13). This means you need to repent—to turn away from sin and turn to God, and believe—to trust in Jesus who died and rose again. He will forgive your sins. Then you will be a new creature, changed by God our Creator and Savior.

The Maker's Gifts

Who taught the spider how to make
Her silken web so light?
Who gave her such a **cunning** way
To take her **airy** flight?

Who told the **timid** little bird
To play that she was lame,
And try to lead me far away
When near her young I came?

Who taught the little mother wasp
To make her paper nest,
And work away the summer hours
Without a thought of rest?

How does a little honey bee
Know how to make her cell,
And fill it with such **dainty** food
To feed her babies well?

It was their Maker gave to them
Such **wondrous skillful** ways;
He gives them all some work to do
Through all the summer days.

He gives to us, my children dear,
More skill of mind and heart;
Let us then praise Jesus Christ
And always do our part.

—Author Unknown

All Things

All things bright and beautiful,
All creatures great and small,
All things wise and wonderful,
The Lord God made them all.

Each little flower that opens,
Each little bird that sings,
He made their glowing colors,
He made their tiny wings.

—*Mrs. C. F. Alexander*

The Boy That Never Sees

God help the boy that never sees
The butterflies, the birds, the bees,
Nor hears the music of the breeze
    When **zephyrs** soft are blowing;

Who can not in sweet comfort lie
Where clover blooms are thick and high,
And hear the gentle murmur nigh
    Of **brooklets** softly flowing.

God help the boy that does not know
Where all the woodland berries grow;
Who never sees the forest's glow
    When leaves are red and yellow;

Whose childish feet can never stray
Where nature doth her charms display—
For such a helpless boy, I say,
    God help the little fellow.

—Author Unknown

A Hymn

"Father, we thank thee for the night,
And for the pleasant morning light,
For rest and food and loving care,
And all that makes the world so fair.

Help us to do the things we should,
To be to others kind and good;
In all we do, in work or play,
To grow more loving every day."

The End

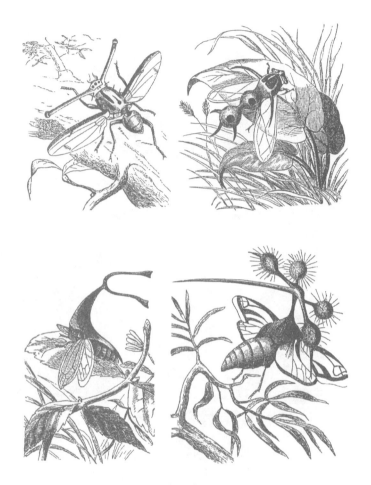

God has protected the strange insects pictured above by making them look like the color and shape of plants. Do you remember what this is called?

Words You Should Know

A

Airy—in the air; light as air

Antelope—deerlike animals that are very fast runners, chew their food more than once, and have horns that are empty inside

Antennae—sticklike parts that grow out of an insect's head; they help them smell and are often called *feelers*.

Aphids—small insects that suck sweet juice or *honeydew* from plants

---

B

Beebread—pollen and honey mixed together; it is stored by the bees and fed to their young.

Beehive—a place for a colony of bees to make and store honey

Beetles—insects with mouthparts that are used for biting; they have hard front wings which cover their soft, thin back wings when they are closed.

Bison—animals that look like cows but have hairy necks, short curved horns, and a humped back; the American buffalo

Blossoms—flowers on a plant that grows fruit

Brooklets—small streams of water; little brooks

Burrow—a hole or tunnel dug in the ground by an animal

C

Caddisfly—an insect that has two pairs of hairy wings

Caddisworm—the larva of the caddis fly; it lives in the water and protects itself by building a case of sand, tiny stones, bits of shell, or small plant parts.

Camouflage—changing the way a person or thing looks to hide from, or mislead, an enemy

Carpenter bees—solitary bees that make their nests in solid wood; they drill long tunnels in wood and make rooms, or *cells*; they lay their eggs in these cells

Cell—a small room built by an insect for laying eggs and storing food

Chemical—material that causes a change when it is mixed with a different material

Chorus—a group of singers that perform together

Chrysalis—the pupa of a moth or butterfly; also the name of the hard shell that covers the moth or butterfly during the pupa stage

Cicada—a large, flylike insect that has clear wings; as a nymph it feeds on the roots of trees for seventeen years; the adult male makes a loud, sharp sound that is repeated very fast.

Claws—the sharp nails on the foot of an animal

Cocoon—the silky case that the larvae of many insects spin around themselves; this case protects them during the pupa stage

Colony—a group of insects that live and grow together

Commandments—the Ten Commandments (Exodus 20:1-17 and Deuteronomy 5:6-22) and all other laws or commands that God has given in His Word, the Bible

Computer—an instrument that can add and subtract very fast, and do other things that used to take a long time to do; it also carries sounds and pictures from one place to another; it uses electricity to work.

Concert—a program with singers and musicians

Covenant—a relationship that God sets up with us and backs it up by His word

Coyote—a small wolf that lives on the western prairies of North America

Creation—all that God has made in the beginning, by the word of His power; He created the world out of nothing within six days, and it was all very good.

Creatures—all living things created by God that move across the earth

Cuckoo bee—a bee that lays its eggs in a bumblebee hive; the bumblebees are tricked and end up raising the cuckoo bee's young.

Cunning—made or done with great skill; skillful or clever

Curse—the evil that God sends upon a person or a group of people for disobeying His Word

Cuttlefish—squidlike sea animals that have ten arms covered with suckers, and a hard inner shell; when in danger some give off a dark brown, ink-like liquid to help them get away from their enemies

D

Dainty—something that is very fine and beautiful, and can be easily damaged

Dam—anything that is built to stop the flow of water in a stream, river, or body of water

Delicate—beautiful, fine, and easily broken or damaged

Digger wasps—wasps that dig in the earth to lay their eggs; they live and work alone.

Diver—a person or animal that jumps head first into the water

Dragonflies—large insects that have narrow, clear wings; their two pairs of wings are always at right angles to their bodies, even at rest; they are not harmful but help by eating flies and mosquitoes.

Drone—the male bee that mates with the queen; it does not work and has no sting.

E

Earthworms—worms that have long, round bodies that are divided into many ringlike parts; they dig in the soil and feed on tiny bits of food.

Earwig—long insects that have short, horny front wings, and mouthparts used for biting; at the rear end of their bodies, they have a pair of large, jawlike tools for holding things.

Egyptians—people that lived in North Africa along the Nile River in Bible times; the Israelites became their slaves after the death of Joseph around 1700 B.C.

Electricity—power made of very tiny *charges* that flow in wires, and is used to run *electrical* machines and products

Enemy—a person or thing that tries to hurt or harm another

F

Feelers—special parts of an insect that helps it feel or smell, such as *antennae*

Females—women or girls

Ferns—plants that have leaves called *fronds* or branch-like leaves with many small leaves attached to a stem

Fireflies—beetles that have wings and soft bodies; their back ends give off natural light which they create without making heat; their larvae and wingless females are called *glowworms.*

Fleas—small insects that have flat bodies, large legs for jumping, and no wings; adult fleas suck blood from *mammals* and birds. [Mammals are warm-blooded animals with hairy bodies.]

Fur—thick, hairy skin of warm-blooded animals, such as bears, foxes, deer, monkeys, lions, etc.

G

Gall—a small ball that grows on the leaves or stems of plants; this is caused by a special *chemical* left by the gallfly

Gallfly—a fly who lays its eggs on leaves or stems of plants; the eggs or larvae cause *galls* to form

Germs—a very small animal or plant that can make a person sick; these tiny living things can only be seen with a *microscope.*

Gnaw—to cut, bite, and wear away little by little with the teeth

God—the Maker of everything; there is only one true God; He is a Spirit and does not have a body as we do; God is One, yet He is three Persons: God the Father, God the Son, and God the Holy Spirit—the *Trinity.* [1]

Greedy—wanting more and more food or drink

Grub—the short, fat, wormlike larva of an insect

H

Harmful—something that hurts or damages a person, place, or thing

Hatch—to come out of an egg

Hawk—birds of prey that have a hooked beak, short rounded wings, and a long tail

Hawkmoths—moths with thick, fuzzy bodies; long, thin wings; and long, tubelike mouths. They fly very fast, and hover when sipping nectar from flowers.

Hibernate—to sleep through the winter

Hinge—the part that holds a door to the house

Holy Spirit—the third person of the *Trinity*: God the Father, God the Son, and God the Holy Spirit; the Spirit of God is the Giver of Life.

---

1. Adapted from *Catechism For Young Children*, published by Great Commission Publications.

Honey ants—ants that collect nectar and honeydew from plants and other insects, and store it in special worker ants called *repletes*

Honey bee—a bee that makes and stores honey; a common insect that lives in a beehive

Honeycomb—a place made by the bees to store honey and eggs; it is made up of many cells, or tiny rooms, that have six sides each.

Honeydew—a sweet liquid that is sucked out of different kinds of plants by *aphids* and other such insects

Human—having to do with a person, not an animal, plant, or thing; a general name for a boy or girl, man or woman

Hummingbirds—very small American birds that are brightly colored; they have long, thin bills for drinking nectar, and narrow wings that move back and forth very fast, often with a humming sound.

I

Ichneumon fly—insects whose larvae feed on other insect larvae; ichneumon means *tracker*.

Image—someone or something that looks just like another

Invention—something new that a person thought of and then built; something that makes work easier, faster, or better

---

J

Jesus Christ—the second person of the *Trinity*: God the Father, God the Son, and God the Holy Spirit; Jesus is the Creator and Savior of the world.

K

Kingbirds—birds called American flycatchers; they have grayish-black feathers and a white-tipped tail

L

Larvae—small baby insects that hatch from eggs; these wormlike creatures are sometimes called grubs, caterpillars, or maggots; *larva*, singular of larvae

Leaf-cutter bees—bees that cut circle-shaped pieces from leaves or flowers to make their nests

Locust—grasshoppers that have short antennae and commonly travel in swarms

Loopers—larvae of moths that move by looping their bodies; first they move the front end of their bodies and then bring up their back end to make a loop; they are also called *measuring worms.*

M

Males—men or boys

Markings—special marks or coloring that belong to an animal or plant

Mate—the husband or wife of a person or animal

Mayflies—insects with soft, delicate bodies and thin, clear wings; mayfly larvae live several years in the water, but adult mayflies live only hours or a few days.

Meadow—a piece of grassland that is used for feeding cattle or sheep or for growing hay

Metamorphosis—the four stages of growth of most insects: the egg, the larva, the pupa, and the adult

Microscope—an instrument that uses pieces of glass to help a person see very tiny things

Molting—throwing off the old outer skin as the insect's new skin grows under the old

Moths—insects that have four fuzzy wings and fly at night; smaller and less colorful than butterflies

Mud wasps—wasps that make their houses out of mud; they work alone; mud daubers, potter wasps, etc.

N

Nectar—sweet liquid found in many flowers; it is used by bees to make honey.

Nymphs—young insects that look a lot like their parents when they are born; dragonflies, mayflies, and grasshoppers are a few that go through *incomplete metamorphosis* (egg, nymph, and adult stages).

O

Orchestra—a group that plays musical instruments together

P

Paper wasps—wasps that make their houses out of paper-like material and live in colonies; hornets, yellow jackets, etc.

Perch—a place where a bird rests, usually high on a tree branch or power line

Pharaoh—the title given to the rulers of Egypt during Bible times

Planet—a heavenly body that looks like a ball and moves around the sun; the nine planets that move around the sun are: *Mercury, Venus, Earth, Mars, Jupiter, Saturn, Uranus, Neptune, Pluto.*

Pocket gophers—animals that dig holes in the ground; they are the size of large rats and have pockets in their cheeks

Pollen—yellow, powderlike cells found on flowers

Prairie—a large area of grassland that is nearly flat or a bit rolling

Prey—an animal hunted or killed for food by another animal

Pupae—insects that stop feeding, make a covering, and rest so they can change into adults; *pupa,* singular of pupae

---

Q

Quail—small game birds that have short beaks and noses protected by scales; they nest in grass and lay ten to fifteen white eggs at a time.

Queen—the female insect in a colony of bees, ants, or termites that mates and lays eggs

---

R

Replete—a special honey ant that has the job of storing honeydew inside its body in a part called the *gaster*

Rocket ship—a spaceship that has rockets to take it into outer space; these rockets have air (oxygen) and fuel inside them; when they are mixed together and burned they make the ship move in space.

S

Sac—a small pocket that is part of a animal or plant

Scales—thin, hard plates that are flat or toothlike, and cover the body of a fish

Shell—the hard outer covering of a turtle, oyster, insect, or egg

Shrill—a very high, sharp sound that hurts the ears

Silk—the threadlike material made by a spider or insect

Sin—any thought, word, or deed that breaks God's law

Skill—a special ability to do something well; this ability comes from talent, training, or practice

Skillful—having or showing *skill*; having much training and knowledge in some special work; also spelled *skilful*

Skin—the outer covering of a person or animal

Snails—slow-moving animals that live on the land or in the water; they carry their houses, or *shells*, with them on their backs; they have only one foot on which they move.

Social—living and working together

Solitary—living and working alone

Soul—the spiritual part of a person that never dies; this part controls what a person thinks, says, and does.

Spin—make silk thread; a spider or insect *spins* by pushing out a liquid that hardens in the air

Spinnerets—small parts of a spider or insect that spin the silky threads

Submarine—a ship that can dive and move under water; often used as a warship

Swarm—a large number of bees, led by a queen, who are leaving the hive to start a new colony

---

T

Telephone—an instrument that carries sounds and words from one place to another; it uses electricity to work.

Telescope—an instrument that uses pieces of glass to help a person see things far away

Television—an instrument that carries sounds and pictures from one place to another; it uses electricity to work.

Timid—easily frightened; not sure of oneself; shy

Tomato worm—the large, green larva of the hawkmoth; this caterpillar feeds on tomato plants.

Tracker—an animal that carefully follows the *tracks* or footprints of another animal for food; a hunter

Trapdoor—a door that is hidden; also the name of spiders that make trapdoors over the openings of their houses

Trowel—a tool that has a flat blade with a handle; it is used to put plaster or similar material on wood, stone, or brick

Tumblebugs—beetles that roll balls of dung and bury them in the soil; female tumblebugs lay their eggs in or on these balls; when the larvae hatch they grow up in these balls

Tunnel—a hole made under the ground for animals to live in or lay eggs

---

U

Umbrella—a round piece of cloth pulled over a set of wires that branch out from the center of a post that looks like the letter "J"; it is used to keep the rain or sun away

---

W

Walking sticks—insects that have long, sticklike bodies with no wings; they feed on plants.

Wax—solid, yellow material that is made by bees to build the cells of a honeycomb

Weather—what the air is like outside at a certain time and place (hot or cold, wet or dry)

Webbed—having the fingers or toes connected by a web-like material

Web—the threads of a spider or insect that are spun to look like a net

Wigglers—larvae of mosquitoes that *wiggle* as they swim through the water

Wisdom—what has to do with being *wise*; using what you know in the best way; knowing the difference between good and evil, right and wrong, and using what you know to honor God

Wondrous—filled with *wonder*; causing praise to God for what He has done

Workers—females that do the work in a colony of bees, ants, or termites

Worth—how helpful or important a person or thing is to someone or something else

---

Z

Zephyr—the west wind; a soft, gentle breeze